The Mystery of the Eucharist in the Life of the Church

OSV

Our Sunday Visitor
Huntington, Indiana

The document *The Mystery of the Eucharist in the Life of the Church* was developed by the Committee on Doctrine of the United States Conference of Catholic Bishops (USCCB). It was approved by the full body of the USCCB at its November 2021 General Meeting and has been authorized for publication by the undersigned.

Rev. Michael J. K. Fuller
General Secretary, USCCB

ISBN: 978-1-63966-292-0 (Inventory T2951)
eISBN: 978-1-63966-293-7

First printing, January 2022
Current printing, 2024, published by OSV, Our Sunday Visitor, 200 Noll Plaza, Huntington, IN 46750; 1-800-348-2440; www.osv.com.

Cover image: *The Institution of the Eucharist* by Ercole de' Roberti, National Gallery, London (public domain image)

PRINTED IN THE UNITED STATES OF AMERICA

1. On March 27, 2020, at an early point in the global pandemic, Pope Francis walked alone in the rain across an empty St. Peter's Square to offer prayer for the world in a time of crisis. "Faith," he said, "begins when we realize we are in need of salvation. We are not self-sufficient; by ourselves we founder: we need the Lord, like ancient navigators needed the stars."[1] Recalling when Jesus was asleep in the boat as a tempest was raging (Mk 4:35-41), the Holy Father said, "The Lord awakens so as to reawaken and revive our Easter faith."[2] On that day, Pope Francis presided over the rite of Eucharistic Exposition and Benediction in order to focus our attention on the presence of Christ in the Blessed Sacrament. The Pope was reminding us that even in a time of turbulence and crisis, Jesus is present among us, as present as he was long ago in the boat on the Sea of Galilee.

2. In similar fashion, Pope Saint John Paul II reminded us of this ongoing presence when he repeated to us the words of Christ: *I am with you*

---

1 Pope Francis, *Extraordinary Moment of Prayer*, March 27, 2020 (*https://www.vatican.va/content/francesco/en/messages/urbi/documents/papa-francesco_20200327_urbi-et-orbi-epidemia.html*).

2 Pope Francis, *Extraordinary Moment of Prayer*, March 27, 2020.

always, to the end of the age (Mt 28:20). He proclaimed: "This promise of Christ never ceases to resound in the Church as the fertile secret of her life and the wellspring of her hope. As the day of Resurrection, Sunday is not only the remembrance of a past event: it is a celebration of the living presence of the Risen Lord in the midst of his own people."[3]

3. We call on these inspiring words of the saintly Pope John Paul II as we offer these reflections on the importance of the Eucharist in the life of the Church. We do so mindful of how the pandemic has forced us to stay physically distant from one another and, for a time, to view the celebration of the Mass on a television or computer screen. Many of the faithful appear to have had their faith and their desire for the Eucharist strengthened by such a long separation. At the same time, as pastors we sense that others, having lived without Mass for so long, may have become discouraged or accustomed to life without the Eucharist. In many ways the pandemic is still with us.

3 Pope John Paul II, *Dies Domini*, no. 31.

4. As Christians we know that we need Christ to be present in our lives. He is our very sustenance as he reminded us: *unless you eat the flesh of the Son of Man and drink his blood, you do not have life within you* (Jn 6:53).

5. The Lord accompanies us in many ways, but none as profound as when we encounter him in the Eucharist. On our journey toward eternal life, Christ nourishes us with his very self. Once, when told by someone that she no longer saw the point of going to daily Mass, the Servant of God Dorothy Day reflected: "We go eat of this fruit of the tree of life because Jesus told us to. . . . He took upon himself our humanity that we might share in his divinity. We are nourished by his flesh that we may grow to be other Christs. I believe this literally, just as I believe the child is nourished by the milk from his mother's breast."[4]

---

4 *The Duty of Delight: The Diaries of Dorothy Day*, ed. Robert Ellsberg (New York: Image, 2011) p. 483; see *Roman Missal*, Collect for the Nativity of the Lord, Mass during the Day: "O God, who wonderfully created the dignity of human nature and still more wonderfully restored it, grant, we pray, that we may share in the divinity of Christ, who humbled himself to share in our humanity."

6. Yet, we also know that he is present to us in a way that binds us together as one body, which we proclaim by our "Amen" in responding to the invitation: The Body of Christ. Again, we call on the words of the beloved Polish pope: "For this presence to be properly proclaimed and lived, it is not enough that the disciples of Christ pray individually and commemorate the death and Resurrection of Christ inwardly, in the secrecy of their hearts. Those who have received the grace of baptism are not saved as individuals alone, but as members of the Mystical Body, having become part of the People of God."[5]

7. As we continue to welcome people back to the communal celebration of the Mass, it must be acknowledged that no document can exhaust the mystery of the gift of the Eucharist. Nevertheless, at various times, it is desirable to reflect on certain facets of the mystery that are relevant to contemporary issues and challenges and that help us to appreciate more deeply the gift of grace that has been given to us. At this particular moment for the Church in the United States, with its many challenges, we

---

5 Pope John Paul II, *Dies Domini*, no. 31.

would like to reflect on Christ's **gift** of himself in the Eucharist and our **response** to that gift.

I. THE GIFT

8. At the Mass of the Lord's Supper celebrated on Holy Thursday, the priest prays these words:

> For he is the true and eternal Priest,
> who instituted the pattern of an
> everlasting sacrifice
> and was the first to offer himself as the
> saving Victim,
> commanding us to make this offering as
> his memorial.
>
> As we eat his flesh that was sacrificed for us,
> we are made strong,
> and, as we drink his Blood that was poured
> out for us,
> we are washed clean.

The words of the liturgy on the night the Church commemorates the institution of the Eucharist speak to us of the Mass as the re-presentation of Christ's unique sacrifice on the Cross, the reception of Christ truly present in the Sacrament of the Eucharist, and the marvelous effects of communion in those who receive this gift.[6]

9. The mission of the Lord's entire life on earth was to glorify the Father by bringing us salvation. In the Nicene Creed recited at Mass, we profess "For us men and for our salvation he came down from heaven, and by the Holy Spirit was incarnate of the Virgin Mary, and became man." The salvation offered in the Life, Death, and Resurrection of Christ is nothing less than sharing in the very life of God, in the communion of love among the Father, the Son, and the Holy Spirit. There is no greater gift that God could possibly give us. In Christ, we are *sharers in the divine nature* (2 Pt 1:4). The Church Fathers referred to this participation in the divine life as "divinization." The eternal Son of God made this possible by becoming man and uniting humanity to his divine Person. St. Augustine explained, "the maker of man was made man, so that man might be a receiver of

6 See *Roman Missal*, Prayer over the Offerings for Holy Thursday/Second Sunday in Ordinary Time: "Grant us, O Lord, we pray, that we may participate worthily in these mysteries, for whenever the memorial of this sacrifice is celebrated the work of our redemption is accomplished. Through Christ our Lord."

God."[7] In fact, Pope Francis reminds us that "in the bread of the Eucharist, 'creation is projected towards divinization, towards the holy wedding feast, towards unification with the Creator himself.'"[8]

A. The Sacrifice of Christ

10. To begin to comprehend the tremendous gift offered by Christ through his Incarnation, Death, and Resurrection, that gift that is made present to us in the Eucharist, we must first realize how truly profound is our alienation from the Source of all life as a result of sin. We have abundant experience of evil, yet so many of us deny the cause of much of that evil—our own selfishness, our own sins. As St. John wrote in his first letter, *If we say, "we are without sin," we deceive ourselves, and the truth is not in us* (1 Jn 1:8).

11. Sin is an offense against God, a failure to love God and our neighbor that wounds our nature and

---

7 St. Augustine, *Sermon* 23B.1, in *Newly Discovered Sermons*, trans. Edmund Hill, *Works of Saint Augustine*, pt. III (Homilies), vol. 11 (Hyde Park, NY: New City Press, 1997), 37.

8 Pope Francis, *Laudato Si'*, no. 236, citing Pope Benedict XVI, Homily on the Solemnity of the Sacred Body and Blood of Christ (June 15, 2006).

injures human solidarity.[9] The capabilities, talents, and gifts we have received from God are meant to be used for good—not the false and illusory good that we in our self-centered desire create for ourselves, but the true good that glorifies the Father of goodness and is directed for the good of others and, in the end, is also good for us. When we misuse the gifts of creation, when we selfishly focus on ourselves, we choose the path of vice rather than the way of virtue.[10] This self-centeredness is an inheritance of the Fall of our first parents. Without the grace of Christ received at Baptism, strengthened in Confirmation, and nourished by the Eucharist, this selfishness dominates us.[11]

12. In Christ, however, what was lost by sin has been restored and renewed even more wondrously by grace.[12] Jesus, the *new Adam*,[13] "was crucified under Pontius Pilate," offering himself up as a sacrifice so that we may receive the inheritance that was lost

---

9 See *Catechism of the Catholic Church*, nos. 1849-1850.

10 See St. Basil, *Regulae Fusius Tractatae*, Question 2, *Patrologia Graeca* 31:910.

11 See *Catechism of the Catholic Church*, no. 385ff.

12 See *Roman Missal*, Collect for the Nativity of the Lord, Mass during the Day.

13 See 1 Cor 15:45-49.

by sin. By freely offering his life on the cross, Christ allows us to *become the children of God* (Jn 1:12) and to inherit the Kingdom of God.[14] St. Peter reminds us, Christ *himself bore our sins in his body upon the cross, so that, free from sin, we might live for righteousness. By his wounds you have been healed* (1 Pt 2:24).

13. At the Last Supper, celebrating the Passover, Jesus makes explicit that his impending death, freely embraced out of love, is sacrificial: *While they were eating, Jesus took bread, said the blessing, broke it, and giving it to his disciples said, "Take and eat; this is my body." Then he took a cup, gave thanks, and gave it to them, saying, "Drink from it, all of you, for this is my blood of the covenant, which will be shed on behalf of many for the forgiveness of sins"* (Mt 26:27-28). In the words and gestures of the Last Supper, Jesus makes it clear that out of love for us he is freely offering his life for the forgiveness of our sins. In doing so, he is both the priest offering a sacrifice and the victim being offered. As priest, Jesus is offering a sacrifice to God the Father, an offering prefigured by the offering of bread and wine by Melchizedek, Priest of God Most High (Gen 14:18; see Ps 110:4; Heb

14 See Hebrews 9:15; Ephesians 1:14.

5-7 *passim*). Anticipating his Passion in the institution of the Eucharist, Christ has indicated the forms under which his self-offering would be sacramentally present to us until the end of time.

14. Why is it so important that we understand the Eucharist as a sacrifice? It is because all that Jesus did for the salvation of humanity is made present in the celebration of the Eucharist, including his sacrificial Death and Resurrection. Christ's sacrifice of himself to the Father was efficacious and salvific because of the supreme love with which he shed his blood, the price of our salvation, and offered himself to the Father on our behalf.[15] His blood, shed for us, is the eternal sign of that love. As a memorial the Eucharist is not another sacrifice, but the re-presentation of the sacrifice of Christ by which we are reconciled to the Father.[16] It is the way by which we are drawn into Jesus' perfect offering of love, so that his sacrifice becomes the sacrifice of the Church.[17] As Pope Benedict XVI wrote,

---

15 See Pope Benedict XVI, *Sacramentum Caritatis*, no. 10.

16 See Council of Trent, Session 22, *Doctrine on the Sacrifice of the Mass*, chapter 1.

17 See Pope Benedict XVI, *Sacramentum Caritatis*, no. 10, and *Catechism of the Catholic Church*, no. 1368.

The remembrance of his perfect gift consists not in the mere repetition of the Last Supper, but in the Eucharist itself, that is, in the radical newness of Christian worship. In this way, Jesus left us the task of entering into his "hour." "The Eucharist draws us into Jesus' act of self-oblation. More than just statically receiving the incarnate *Logos*, we enter into the very dynamic of his self-giving."[18]

15. The Eucharist is a sacrificial meal, "the sacred banquet of communion with the Lord's body and blood."[19] Its fundamental pattern is found in the Jewish celebration of the Passover, which involves *both* a meal *and* a sacrifice. The Passover meal is celebrated in remembrance of the Exodus, when the Israelites were told to sacrifice a lamb to the Lord and to mark the doorposts of their houses with the blood, so that the angel of death would pass over their houses and leave the Israelites unharmed. This marked a people set apart and chosen by God as his special possession. Each family was then to eat the lamb with unleavened bread as a reminder of the

---

18 Pope Benedict XVI, *Sacramentum Caritatis*, no. 11, quoting *Deus Caritas Est*, no. 13.

19 *Catechism of the Catholic Church*, no. 1382.

haste with which the Israelites had to prepare for their departure from Egypt and with bitter herbs as a reminder of their deliverance from slavery. At the Last Supper, Jesus reveals himself to be the Paschal Lamb ("Behold the Lamb of God") whose sacrifice brings liberation from slavery to sin and whose blood marks out a new people belonging to God. All the sacrifices in the Old Testament prefigure and find their fulfillment in the one perfect sacrifice of Jesus.

16. The saving work of Jesus Christ, which has brought to fulfillment what was announced in figure in the Passover, is now re-presented in the celebration of the Eucharist. The Eucharist "makes present the one sacrifice of Christ the Savior."[20] As Pope St. John Paul II taught: "The Church constantly draws her life from [this] redeeming sacrifice; she approaches it not only through faith-filled remembrance, but also through a real contact, since *this sacrifice is made present ever anew*, sacramentally perpetuated, in every community which offers it at the hands of the consecrated minister."[21]

---

20 *Catechism of the Catholic Church*, no. 1330.

21 Pope John Paul II, *Ecclesia de Eucharistia*, no. 12.

17. Finally, this great sacrament is also a participation in the worship offered in heaven, in and through Christ, by the angels and saints. Pope Benedict XVI explained that

> every eucharistic celebration sacramentally accomplishes the eschatological gathering of the People of God. For us, the eucharistic banquet is a real foretaste of the final banquet foretold by the prophets (cf. Is 25:6-9) and described in the New Testament as "the marriage-feast of the Lamb" (Rev 19:7-9), to be celebrated in the joy of the communion of saints.[22]

B. The Real Presence of Christ

18. From the very beginning, the Church has believed and celebrated according to the teaching of Jesus himself: *Whoever eats my flesh and drinks my blood has eternal life and I will raise him on the last day. For my flesh is true food, and my blood is true drink. Whoever eats my flesh and drinks my blood remains in me and I in him* (Jn 6:54-56). It is not "ordinary bread and ordinary drink" that we receive in the Eucharist,

22 Pope Benedict XVI, *Sacramentum Caritatis*, no. 31.

but the flesh and blood of Christ, who came to nourish and transform us, to restore our relationship to God and to one another.[23]

19. In the Eucharist, with the eyes of faith we see before us Jesus Christ, who, in the Incarnation *became flesh* (Jn 1:14) and who in the Paschal Mystery *gave himself for us* (Ti 2:14), accepting *even death on a cross* (Phil 2:8). St. John Chrysostom preached that when you see the Body of Christ "set before you [on the altar], say to yourself: Because of this Body I am no longer earth and ashes, no longer a prisoner, but free: because of this I hope for heaven, and to receive the good things therein, immortal life, the portion of angels, [and closeness] with Christ."[24]

20. How can Jesus Christ be truly present in what still appears to be bread and wine? In the liturgical act known as the epiclesis, the bishop or priest, speaking in the person of Jesus Christ, calls upon the Father to send down his Holy Spirit to change the bread and wine into the Body and Blood of Christ, and this change occurs through the institution

23 See St. Justin Martyr, *First Apology*, LXVI.

24 St. John Chrysostom, *Homilies on First Corinthians*, 24.7, in *Nicene and Post-Nicene Fathers*, First series (Peabody, MA: Hendrickson, 1995), 142.

narrative, by the power of the words of Christ pronounced by the celebrant.[25]

21. The reality that, in the Eucharist, bread and wine become the Body and Blood, Soul and Divinity of Christ without ceasing to appear as bread and wine to our five senses is one of the central mysteries of the Catholic faith. This faith is a doorway through which we, like the saints and mystics before us, may enter into a deeper perception of the mercy and love manifested in and through Christ's sacramental presence in our midst. While one thing is seen with our bodily eyes, another reality is perceived through the eyes of faith. The real, true, and substantial presence of Christ in the Eucharist is the most profound reality of the sacrament. "This mysterious change is very appropriately called by the Church transubstantiation."[26] Though Christ is present to us in many ways in the liturgy, including in the assembly gathered, the presiding minister, and the word proclaimed, the Church also clearly affirms that "the mode of Christ's presence under the Eucharistic

---

25 *Catechism of the Catholic Church*, no. 1353.

26 Pope Paul VI, *Credo of the People of God*, no. 25; cf. Council of Trent, Session 13, *Decree on the Sacrament of the Eucharist*, ch. 4.

species is unique."[27] As St. Paul VI wrote, "This presence is called 'real' not to exclude the idea that the others are 'real' too, but rather to indicate presence *par excellence*, because it is substantial and through it Christ becomes present whole and entire, God and man."[28] In the sacramental re-presentation of his sacrifice, Christ holds back nothing, offering himself, whole and entire. The use of the word "substantial" to mark the unique presence of Christ in the Eucharist is intended to convey the totality of the gift he offers to us.

22. When the Eucharist is distributed and the minister says, "the Body of Christ," we are to look not simply at what is visible before our eyes, but at what it has become by the words of Christ and the gift of the Holy Spirit—the Body of Christ.[29] The communicant's response of "Amen" is a profession of faith in the Real Presence of Christ and reflects the intimate personal encounter with him, with his gift of self, that comes through reception of Holy Communion.

---

27 *Catechism of the Catholic Church*, no. 1374; see also *Sacrosanctum Concilium*, no.7.

28 Pope Paul VI, *Mysterium Fidei*, no. 39.

29 See St. Irenaeus, *Against Heresies*, IV.16.28.

23. The Church's firm belief in the Real Presence of Christ is reflected in the worship that we offer to the Blessed Sacrament in various ways, including Eucharistic Exposition, Adoration, and Benediction; Eucharistic Processions; and Forty Hours Devotions. In addition, the practices of reverently genuflecting before the Blessed Sacrament reserved in the tabernacle, bowing one's head prior to the reception of Holy Communion, and refraining from food and drink for at least one hour before receiving Communion are clear manifestations of the Church's Eucharistic faith.[30]

C. Communion with Christ and the Church

24. When we receive Holy Communion, Christ is giving himself to us. He comes to us in all humility, as he came to us in the Incarnation, so that we may receive him and become one with him. Christ gives himself to us so that we may continue the pilgrim path toward life with him in the fullness of the Kingdom of God. The fourteenth-century Orthodox

30 See *Code of Canon Law*, can. 919 §1. "A person who is to receive the Most Holy Eucharist is to abstain for at least one hour before holy communion from any food and drink, except for only water and medicine."

theologian Nicholas Cabasilas described this sacrament by saying, "unlike any other sacrament, the mystery [of the Eucharist] is so perfect that it brings us to the heights of every good thing: here is the ultimate goal of every human desire, because here we attain God and God joins himself to us in the most perfect union."[31] Through this sacrament, the pilgrim Church is nourished, deepening her communion with the Triune God and consequently that of her members with one another.[32]

25. The Sacrament of the Eucharist is called Holy Communion precisely because, by placing us in intimate communion with the sacrifice of Christ, we are placed in intimate communion with him and, through him, with each other. Therefore, the Eucharist is called Holy Communion because it is "the efficacious sign and sublime cause of that communion in the divine life and that unity of the People of God by which the Church is kept in being."[33] How can we understand this? The Gospel of John

31 Nicholas Cabasilas, *Life in Christ*, IV.10, quoted in Pope John Paul II, *Ecclesia de Eucharistia*, no. 34.

32 See Pope John Paul II, *Ecclesia de Eucharistia*, no. 34.

33 *Catechism of the Catholic Church*, no. 1325, citing *Eucharisticum Mysterium*, no. 6.

recounts that, when Jesus died on the cross, *blood and water flowed* out (Jn 19:34), symbolic of Baptism and the Eucharist. The Second Vatican Council teaches, "The origin and growth of the Church are symbolized by the blood and water which flowed from the open side of the crucified Jesus,"[34] and that "it was from the side of Christ as he slept the sleep of death upon the cross that there came forth the wondrous sacrament of the whole Church."[35] In this image from the Gospel of John, we see that the Church, the Bride of the Lamb, is born from the sacrificial love of Christ in his self-offering on the cross. The Eucharist re-presents this one sacrifice so that we are placed in communion with it and with the divine love from which it flows forth. We are placed in communion with each other through this love which is given to us. That is why we can say, "the Eucharist makes the Church."[36]

26. We are first incorporated into the Body of Christ, the Church, through the waters of Baptism.[37]

---

34 Second Vatican Council, *Lumen Gentium*, no. 3.
35 Second Vatican Council, *Sacrosanctum Concilium*, no. 5
36 *Catechism of the Catholic Church*, no. 1396.
37 *Code of Canon Law*, c. 849; *Code of Canons of the Eastern Churches*, c. 675 §1.

Yet Baptism, like the other sacraments, is ordered toward Eucharistic communion.[38] The Second Vatican Council teaches,

> The other sacraments, as well as with every ministry of the Church and every work of the apostolate, are tied together with the Eucharist and are directed toward it. The Most Blessed Eucharist contains the entire spiritual boon of the Church, that is, Christ himself, our Pasch and Living Bread, by the action of the Holy Spirit through his very flesh vital and vitalizing, giving life to men who are thus invited and encouraged to offer themselves, their labors and all created things, together with him.

The Council Fathers continue,

> In this light, the Eucharist shows itself as the source and the apex of the whole work of preaching the Gospel. Those under instruction are introduced by stages to a sharing in the Eucharist, and the faithful, already marked with the seal of Baptism and Confirmation, are through the reception of the Eucharist fully

38 *Code of Canon Law*, c. 897.

joined to the Body of Christ.[39]

That is why the Council calls the eucharistic sacrifice "the source and summit of the Christian life."[40]

27. St. Paul emphasizes that this communion exists not only among ourselves but also with those who came before us. In addressing the Church at Corinth, he praises them for holding *fast to the traditions, just as I handed them on to you* (1 Cor 11:2). Later, he highlights the Eucharist as a sacred tradition handed on by Christ to the Apostles, and in which we now share: *For I received from the Lord what I also handed on to you* (1 Cor 11:23). During every Mass we are united with all the holy men and women, the saints, who have preceded us.

28. The obligation to attend Mass each Sunday, the Lord's Day, on which we commemorate the Resurrection of Jesus, and on other holy days of obligation, is therefore a vital expression of our unity as members of the Body of Christ, the Church.[41] It is also a manifestation of the truth that we are utterly

39 Second Vatican Council, *Presbyterorum Ordinis*, no. 5.

40 Second Vatican Council, *Lumen Gentium*, no. 11.

41 *Code of Canon Law*, cc. 1246-1248; *Code of Canons of the Eastern Churches*, c. 881.

dependent upon God and his grace. A third-century instruction on the life of the Church points out one of the consequences of willful absence from Mass: "Let no one deprive the Church by staying away; if they do, they deprive the Body of Christ of one of its members!"[42] St. John Paul II, writing of Sunday as "a day which is at the very heart of the Christian life," further asserts, "Time given to Christ is never time lost, but is rather time gained, so that our relationships and indeed our whole life may become more profoundly human."[43] We have been reborn in Baptism and nourished by the Eucharist so that we may live in communion with God and one another, not only today but also in the fullness of the heavenly Kingdom. To worship God on Sundays, then, is not the mere observance of a rule but the fulfillment of our identity, of who we are as members of the Body of Christ. Participation in the Mass is an act of love.

---

42 *Didascalia Apostolorum*, no. 13.

43 Pope John Paul II, *Dies Domini*, no. 7.

II. OUR RESPONSE

29. In the fourth Common Preface of the *Roman Missal*, the priest prays the following:

> For, although you have no need of our praise, yet our thanksgiving is itself your gift, since our praises add nothing to your greatness but profit us for salvation. . . .

These words speak of the grace of God, the gift freely given, which inspires us to give thanks and worship him, works our transformation into the likeness of Christ, helps us to seek pardon and to receive it when we fall into sin, and impels us to go forth and bear witness to Christ in the world.

A. Thanksgiving and Worship

30. Having been sanctified by the gift of the Eucharist and filled with faith, hope, and charity, the faithful are called to respond to this gift. Indeed, it is only natural that we give thanks to the Lord for all that he has given to us. *How can I repay the Lord for all the great good done for me? I will raise the cup of salvation and call on the name of the Lord* (Ps 116:12).

The word "Eucharist" literally means "thanksgiving." Even our manner of giving thanks comes from God, for we do so by following the command of the Lord: *do this in memory of me* (Lk 22:19).

31. The Second Vatican Council taught that, in order to give thanks properly in the celebration of the Mass, we should "take a full, conscious, and active part in the liturgical celebration."[44] We need to be conscious of the gift we have received, a gift that is none other than the Lord himself in his act of self-giving. We become conscious of this gift when we actively engage our minds, hearts, and bodies to every part of the liturgy, allowing God through the words, actions, gestures, and even the moments of silence to speak to us. We actively and consciously participate by giving our full attention to the words being spoken in the prayers and the Scriptures, even if we have heard them hundreds of times before. We do so also by listening to the homily and reflecting upon how the Lord may be speaking to us through his ordained minister. We are actively giving thanks when we join in singing and in the responses; when

44 Second Vatican Council, *Sacrosanctum Concilium*, no. 14; see also *Code of Canon Law*, cc. 835 §4 and 837 §2, and *Code of Canons of the Eastern Churches*, c. 673.

we kneel, stand, and sit; and when we pay attention to the liturgical seasons where the entire history of what God has done for us, in and through his Son, is revealed to us.

32. The gratitude that inspires us to give thanks and worship God in the celebration of the Eucharist should be nurtured and enriched by the beauty of the liturgical action itself. Bishops and priests have a particular duty to ensure that the Mass is celebrated in a manner befitting the sacredness of what takes place. As Pope Francis recently wrote to the bishops of the world, "I ask you to be vigilant in ensuring that every liturgy be celebrated with decorum and fidelity to the liturgical books promulgated after Vatican Council II, without the eccentricities that can easily degenerate into abuses."[45] Priest celebrants of the Mass should have a prayerful understanding of the liturgical books, as well as of the feasts and seasons, and be faithful to the texts and rubrics established by the Church.[46] In doing so, they will lead the people

---

45 Pope Francis, Letter to the Bishops of the Whole World, That Accompanies the Apostolic Letter *Motu Proprio Data "Traditionis Custodes,"* July 16, 2021.

46 *Code of Canon Law*, c. 846 §1; *Code of Canons of the Eastern Churches*, c. 668 §2.

more deeply and reverently into the exchange that is the dialogue of the Father and the Son in the Holy Spirit.[47]

33. Our gratitude is also expressed in our worship of the Blessed Sacrament outside of Mass. These forms of worship are all intrinsically related to the Eucharistic celebration.

> In the Eucharist, the Son of God comes to meet us and desires to become one with us; eucharistic adoration is simply the natural consequence of the eucharistic celebration. Receiving the Eucharist means adoring him whom we receive. Only in this way do we become one with him, and are given, as it were, a foretaste of the beauty of the heavenly liturgy.[48]

We rejoice in the growing numbers of the faithful who pray in adoration before the Blessed Sacrament, a testament of faith in the Real Presence of the Lord in the Eucharist. We encourage this devotion, which helps all of us to be formed by the self-giving love we behold in the Lord's gift of himself in the Eucharist.

---

47 See *https://www.usccb.org/prayer-and-worship/the-mass/frequently-asked-questions/ars-celebrandi*.

48 Pope Benedict XVI, *Sacramentum Caritatis*, no. 66.

St. (Mother) Teresa of Calcutta reportedly once said: "When you look at the crucifix, you understand how much Jesus loved you then. When you look at the Sacred Host, you understand how much Jesus loves you now."

B. Transformation in Christ

34. The person who shares worthily in the Eucharist is enabled more and more to live the new law of love given by Christ precisely because Christ communicates himself in the sacrament of the altar. The foundation of our personal and moral transformation is the communion with himself that Christ establishes in Baptism and deepens in the Eucharist. In the celebration of the Mass, we are shown what love truly is, and we receive grace that enables us to imitate the love that Christ shows us. St. John Paul II noted that the moral life of the Christian flows from and is nourished by "that inexhaustible source of holiness and glorification of God" that is found in the sacraments, especially the Eucharist: "by sharing in the sacrifice of the Cross, the Christian partakes of Christ's self-giving love and is equipped

and committed to live this same charity in all his thoughts and deeds."[49]

35. The personal and moral transformation that is sustained by the Eucharist reaches out to every sphere of human life. The love of Christ can permeate all of our relationships: with our families, our friends, and our neighbors. It can also reshape the life of our society as a whole. Our relationship with Christ is not restricted to the private sphere; it is not for ourselves alone. The very solidarity or communion in Christ's self-giving love that makes the Church and makes us members of the Church orders us beyond the visible community of faith to all human beings, whom we are to love with that very same love that forms our communion with the Lord. Otherwise, if we do not love all human beings in this way, our communion with the Lord is impaired or even contradicted. This love extends particularly and "preferentially" to the poor and the most vulnerable. We all need to be consistent in bringing the love of Christ not only to our personal lives, but also to every dimension of our public lives.

---

49 Pope John Paul II, *Veritatis Splendor*, no. 107.

36. It is the role of the laity in particular to transform social relations in accord with the love of Christ, which is carried out concretely in actions that work for the objective common good. Lay people, "conscious of their call to holiness by virtue of their baptismal vocation, have to act as leaven in the dough to build up a temporal city in keeping with God's project. [Consistency] between faith and life in the political, economic, and social realm[s] requires formation of conscience, which translates into knowing the Church's social doctrine."[50] Lay people who exercise some form of public authority have a special responsibility to form their consciences in accord with the Church's faith and the moral law, and to serve the human family by upholding human life and dignity.

37. The *Catechism of the Catholic Church* reminds us that the "Eucharist commits us to the poor. To receive in truth the Body and Blood of Christ given up for us, we must recognize Christ in the poorest,

50 V General Conference of the Bishops of Latin America and the Caribbean, *The Aparecida Document*, no. 505; see also *Code of Canon Law*, cc. 225 §2 and 227, and *Code of Canons of the Eastern Churches*, cc. 401-402 and 406.

his brethren."[51] Preaching on Matthew 25, St. John Chrysostom observed: "Do you wish to honor the body of Christ? Do not ignore him when he is naked. Do not pay him homage in the temple clad in silk only then to neglect him outside where he suffers cold and nakedness. He who said: 'This is my body' is the same One who said: 'You saw me hungry and you gave me no food.'"[52] St. Teresa of Calcutta is an outstanding example in more recent times of someone who learned to recognize Christ in the poor. It was her deep faith in the Eucharist and her reception of Holy Communion that motivated her loving care of the poorest of the poor and commitment to the sanctity of all human life. In beholding the face of Christ in the Eucharist, she learned to recognize his face in the poor and suffering. Mother Teresa is said to have asserted: "We must pray to Jesus to give us that tenderness of the Eucharist. Unless we believe and see Jesus in the appearance of bread on the altar, we will not be able to see him in the distressing disguise of the poor."

---

51 *Catechism of the Catholic Church*, no. 1397.

52 St. John Chrysostom, *Homilies on the Gospel of Matthew*, 50, 3-4: *PG* 58, 508-509, as cited by Pope John Paul II in *Dies Domini*, no. 71.

38. Pope Francis has warned us that in our "throwaway culture" we need to fight the tendency to view people as "disposable":

> Some parts of our human family, it appears, can be readily sacrificed for the sake of others considered worthy of a carefree existence. Ultimately, "persons are no longer seen as a paramount value to be cared for and respected, especially when they are poor and disabled, 'not yet useful'—like the unborn, or 'no longer needed'—like the elderly."[53]

As Christians, we bear the responsibility to promote the life and dignity of the human person, and to love and to protect the most vulnerable in our midst: the unborn, migrants and refugees, victims of racial injustice, the sick and the elderly.

39. The Second Vatican Council stresses the importance of reverence toward the human person. "Everyone must consider his every neighbor without exception as another self, taking into account first of all his life and the means necessary to living it with

53 Pope Francis, *Fratelli Tutti*, no. 18, citing his Address to the Diplomatic Corps Accredited to the Holy See (January 11, 2016).

dignity, so as not to imitate the rich man who had no concern for the poor man Lazarus."[54] The Council goes on to say that

> whatever is opposed to life itself, such as any type of murder, genocide, abortion, euthanasia or willful self-destruction, whatever violates the integrity of the human person, such as mutilation, torments inflicted on body or mind, attempts to coerce the will itself; whatever insults human dignity, such as subhuman living conditions, arbitrary imprisonment, deportation, slavery, prostitution, the selling of women and children; as well as disgraceful working conditions, where men are treated as mere tools for profit, rather than as free and responsible persons; all these things and others of their like are infamies indeed. They poison human society, but they do more harm to those who practice them than those who suffer from the injury.[55]

40. Just as we are impelled by the Eucharist to hear the cry of the poor, and respond in love, we are also called to hear the cry of the earth and, likewise,

---

54 Second Vatican Council, *Gaudium et Spes*, no. 27

55 Second Vatican Council, *Gaudium et Spes*, no. 27.

respond with loving care.[56] Pope Francis, like Pope Benedict XVI before him, has eloquently drawn the connection between the celebration of the Eucharist and care for the environment.[57] All creation gives glory to God, and journeys toward divinization, toward union with the Creator.

41. We look forward to the day when all such evils will be eliminated, when the Kingdom of God is established in its fullness. Then, there will be *a new heaven* and *a new earth*, and the human community will dwell in *a new Jerusalem*, in which God himself will dwell with his people (Rev 21:1-3). No one will suffer from poverty or injustice or violence. We will be able to see each other as God sees us, without any of the distortions caused by sin or by structures of sin such as racism or the various manifestations of the throwaway culture. No one will be seen as "disposable." We will be able to love each other in a way that reflects the way God loves us.

42. While it is all too obvious that in our current world the Kingdom has not been fully established, our

56 Pope Francis, *Laudato Si'*, no. 49.

57 Pope Francis, *Laudato Si'*, no. 236; Pope Benedict XVI, *Sacramentum Caritatis*, no. 92.

communion with the Lord shows that the Kingdom of God is not simply something we await at the end of time. The Kingdom is already present, if not in its fullness: "The kingdom has come in the person of Christ and grows mysteriously in the hearts of those incorporated into Him,"[58] until its fulfillment when he comes again in glory. The mystery of the Kingdom remains present in the Church because she is joined to Christ as the members of a Body are to their Head. In the communion which is the Church, "the Kingdom of heaven, the Reign of God, already exists and will be fulfilled at the end of time."[59]

43. God has not only called us out of sinful indifference to do whatever we can to contribute to the coming of the Kingdom; through Christ he has given us the grace we need to do this. The *Compendium of the Social Doctrine of the Church* explains:

> Men and women who are made "new" by the love of God are able to change the rules and the quality of relationships, transforming even social structures. They are people capable of bringing peace where there is conflict, of building and

58 *Catechism of the Catholic Church*, no. 865.

59 *Catechism of the Catholic Church*, no. 865.

nurturing fraternal relationships where there is hatred, of seeking justice where there prevails the exploitation of man by man. Only love is capable of radically transforming the relationships that men maintain among themselves.[60]

C. Conversion

44. Christ began his public ministry by calling people to repentance and conversion: *Repent, and believe in the gospel* (Mk 1:15; cf. Mt 4:17). It is thus fitting that, at the beginning of every Mass, we are invited to acknowledge our sins in order to prepare ourselves to celebrate the sacred mysteries. We confess that we have sinned, and we implore the Lord's mercy. This is necessary since we are all sinners and sometimes fail to live up to our vocation as disciples of Jesus and to the promises of our Baptism. We need continually to heed Christ's call to conversion. We trust in his mercy, the mercy that we behold in his body broken for us and his blood poured out for us for the forgiveness of our sins. We are to approach the Lord with humble and contrite hearts and to say with sincerity: "Lord, I am not worthy that you

60 *Compendium of the Social Doctrine of the Church*, no. 4.

should enter under my roof, but only say the word and my soul shall be healed."

45. While all our failures to do what is right damage our communion with God and with each other, they fall into different categories, reflecting different degrees of severity. This brings us to the distinction between venial and mortal sins. Venial sins are those sins and everyday faults that, although they reflect a degree of selfishness, do not break the covenant with God. They do not deprive the sinner of friendship with God or of sanctifying grace.[61] Venial sins are not to be taken lightly, but they do not destroy communion because they do not destroy the principle of divine life in us. Indeed, reception of the Eucharist strengthens our charity and wipes away venial sins, while also helping us to avoid more serious sins.[62] Pope Francis brought attention to this medicinal character of the Eucharist when he pointed out that it "is not a prize for the perfect but a powerful medicine and nourishment for the weak."[63] He also warns

61 See *Catechism of the Catholic Church*, no. 1863.

62 *Catechism of the Catholic Church*, nos. 1394 and 1395, citing Council of Trent: The Eucharist "is a remedy to free us from our daily faults and to preserve us from mortal sin," Session 13, *Decree on the Sacrament of the Eucharist*, ch. 2.

63 Pope Francis, *Evangelii Gaudium*, no. 47.

us against the Pelagian error of forgetting our constant need for grace and thinking that living a holy life depends on our own force of will.[64]

46. There are some sins, however, that do rupture the communion we share with God and the Church, and that cause grave offense to human dignity. These are referred to as grave, or mortal, sins (see 1 Jn 5:16-17). One commits a mortal sin by freely, knowingly, and willingly choosing to do something that involves grave matter and that is opposed to charity, opposed to love of God and neighbor.[65]

47. One is not to celebrate Mass or receive Holy Communion in the state of mortal sin without having sought the Sacrament of Reconciliation and received absolution.[66] As the Church has consistently taught, a person who receives Holy Communion while in a state of mortal sin not only does not receive the grace that the sacrament conveys; he or she commits the sin of sacrilege by failing to show the reverence due

---

64 Pope Francis, *Gaudete et Exsultate*, nos. 48-62.

65 St. Thomas Aquinas, *Summa Theologiae* I-II, q. 88, art. 2.

66 See *Code of Canon Law*, c. 916; *Code of Canons of the Eastern Churches*, c. 712. The exception to this rule is a situation in which the person has both a grave reason to receive and no opportunity to confess; however, the person is obligated to make an act of perfect contrition and to resolve to confess at the earliest opportunity.

to the sacred Body and Blood of Christ. St. Paul warns us that *whoever eats the bread or drinks the cup of the Lord unworthily will have to answer for the body and blood of the Lord. A person should examine himself, and so eat the bread and drink the cup. For anyone who eats and drinks without discerning the body, eats and drinks judgment on himself* (I Cor 11:27-29). To receive the Body and Blood of Christ while in a state of mortal sin represents a contradiction. The person who, by his or her own action, has broken communion with Christ and his Church but receives the Blessed Sacrament, acts incoherently, both claiming and rejecting communion at the same time. It is thus a counter sign, a lie—it expresses a communion that in fact has been broken.

48. We also need to keep in mind that "the celebration of the Eucharist presupposes that communion already exists, a communion which it seeks to consolidate and bring to perfection."[67] The Eucharist is the sacrament of ecclesial communion, as it both signifies and effects most fully the communion with Christ that began in Baptism. This includes communion in its "visible dimension, which entails communion in the teaching of the Apostles, in the sacraments and

67 Pope John Paul II, *Ecclesia de Eucharistia*, no. 35.

in the Church's hierarchical order."[68] Likewise, the reception of Holy Communion entails one's communion with the Church in this visible dimension. We repeat what the U.S. bishops stated in 2006:

> If a Catholic in his or her personal or professional life were knowingly and obstinately to reject the defined doctrines of the Church, or knowingly and obstinately to repudiate her definitive teaching on moral issues, however, he or she would seriously diminish his or her communion with the Church. Reception of Holy Communion in such a situation would not accord with the nature of the Eucharistic celebration, so that he or she should refrain.[69]

---

68 Pope John Paul II, *Ecclesia de Eucharistia*, no. 35; see also *Code of Canon Law*, c. 205, and *Code of Canons of the Eastern Churches*, c. 8.

69 USCCB, *"Happy Are Those Who Are Called to His Supper": On Preparing to Receive Christ Worthily in the Eucharist*, p. 11; see *Code of Canon Law*, can. 916: "A person who is conscious of grave sin is not to celebrate Mass or receive the body of the Lord without previous sacramental confession unless there is a grave reason and there is no opportunity to confess; in this case the person is to remember the obligation to make an act of perfect contrition which includes the resolution of confessing as soon as possible."

Reception of Holy Communion in such a situation is also likely to cause scandal for others, weakening their resolve to be faithful to the demands of the Gospel.[70]

49. One's communion with Christ and his Church, therefore, involves both one's "invisible communion" (being in the state of grace) and one's "visible communion." St. John Paul II explained:

> The judgment of one's state of grace obviously belongs only to the person involved, since it is a question of examining one's conscience. However, in cases of outward conduct which is seriously, clearly and steadfastly contrary to the moral norm, the Church, in her pastoral concern for the good order of the community and out of respect for the sacrament, cannot fail to feel directly involved. The *Code of Canon Law* refers to this situation of a manifest lack of proper moral disposition when it states that those who 'obstinately persist in manifest grave sin' are not

70 See *Catechism of the Catholic Church*, no. 2284.

to be admitted to Eucharistic communion.[71]

It is the special responsibility of the diocesan bishop to work to remedy situations that involve public actions at variance with the visible communion of the Church and the moral law. Indeed, he must guard the integrity of the sacrament, the visible communion of the Church, and the salvation of souls.

50. Before we receive Holy Communion, we should make a good examination of conscience to ensure that we are properly disposed to receive the Body and Blood of the Lord.[72] If we find that we have broken communion with Christ and his Church, we are not properly disposed to receive the Eucharist. However, we should not despair since the Lord in his mercy has given us a remedy. He loves us and deeply desires to forgive us and to restore our communion with him. On the first Easter night, the Risen

---

71 Pope John Paul II, *Ecclesia de Eucharistia*, no. 37; see *Code of Canon Law*, can. 915: "Those who have been excommunicated or interdicted after the imposition or declaration of the penalty and others obstinately persevering in manifest grave sin are not to be admitted to holy communion." Likewise, the *Code of Canons of the Eastern Churches* states that "those who are publicly unworthy are forbidden from receiving the Divine Eucharist" (c. 712).

72 For the Church's teaching on conscience, see Second Vatican Council, *Gaudium et Spes*, no. 16; *Catechism of the Catholic Church*, nos. 1776-1802, Pope John Paul II, *Veritatis Splendor*, nos. 31-34 and 54-64.

Jesus gave to the Apostles and their successors the power to forgive sins and to reconcile sinners with the Church. He gave the Church the Sacrament of Penance and Reconciliation when he breathed on the Apostles and said to them: *Receive the holy Spirit. Whose sins you forgive are forgiven them, and whose sins you retain are retained* (Jn 20:22-23). Whenever we sin, we have this beautiful opportunity to be renewed and strengthened by God's grace. If we have sinned gravely, the sacrament provides us with the opportunity to recover the gift of sanctifying grace and to be restored to full communion with God and the Church. All the sacrament requires of us as penitents is that we have contrition for our sins, resolve not to sin again, confess our sins, receive sacramental absolution, and do the assigned penance. We encourage all Catholics to a renewed appreciation for this wonderful sacrament in which we receive the Lord's pardon and peace. In the words of Pope Francis, we say to all Catholics in our country: "Don't be afraid to go to the Sacrament of Confession, where you will meet Jesus who forgives you."[73]

73 Pope Francis on Twitter (@Pontifex), December 13, 2013.

D. Food for the Journey

51. The lives of the saints and blesseds show us the importance of the Eucharist on our journey as disciples of Jesus. Many testify to the power of the Eucharist in their lives. We see the fruits of Holy Communion in their lives of faith, hope, and charity. It was their intimate union with Jesus in Holy Communion and frequently their prayer before the Blessed Sacrament that nourished and strengthened them in their journey to heaven. They teach us that "growth in Christian life needs the nourishment of Eucharistic Communion, the bread for our pilgrimage until the moment of death, when it will be given to us as viaticum."[74]

52. Blessed Carlo Acutis, a young Italian teenager, who died at the age of fifteen and was beatified in 2020, used to say: "The Eucharist is my highway to heaven."[75] Blessed Carlo attained sanctity at such a young age because the Eucharist was at the center of his life. He attended Mass daily and prayed

74 *Catechism of the Catholic Church*, no. 1392.

75 See "A Youth of Our Time Captivated by Christ: In Assisi Cardinal Vallini presides on behalf of the Pope over the Beatification of Carlo Acutis," *L'Osservatore Romano* (October 16, 2020).

each day before the Blessed Sacrament in adoration. He discovered the joy of friendship with Jesus and brought that joy, the joy of the Gospel, to others. He was an apostle of the Eucharist through the internet. He said: "To always be united with Christ: This is my life's program."[76]

53. Likewise, St. José Sánchez del Río, a Mexican teenager who was martyred at the age of fourteen and canonized in 2016, was so filled with love of Christ and his Church that he was willing to give up his life rather than renounce Christ and his Kingship. While imprisoned, St. José Sánchez del Río was able to receive the Blessed Sacrament when it was smuggled into his cell along with a basket of food. Strengthened by this viaticum, he was able to endure torture and to remain faithful to Christ when his captors told him he must renounce his faith or be executed.[77] He replied to his persecutors: "My faith is not for sale."[78] We encourage all, especially our young people, to learn about the lives of these

---

76 See Nicola Gori, *Carlo Acutis: The First Millennial Saint*, trans. Daniel Gallagher (Huntington, Ind.: Our Sunday Visitor, 2021), Introduction.

77 See "José Anacleto González Flores and eight Companions—biography," Vatican News Service (November 20, 2005).

78 "Postulator Recalls St. Jose Sanchez del Rio Saying 'My Faith Is Not for Sale,'" *National Catholic Register* (October 17, 2016).

holy teenagers. In the midst of many distractions in our life, Blessed Carlo and St. José Sánchez del Río teach us to focus on what is more important than anything else.

54. There are many people who have been attracted to the Catholic Church and entered the Church because they came to believe in the Real Presence of Christ in the Eucharist. Our first U.S. born saint, Elizabeth Ann Seton, is one of these converts. She was drawn to enter the Catholic Church after she witnessed the devotion of Catholics to the Blessed Sacrament. She wondered about that devotion. God's grace led her to faith in the Real Presence. While still an Episcopalian, she found herself at worship in her church in New York looking out the open window and praying to Jesus in the tabernacle one block away in a Catholic church. On the night after her entrance into the Catholic Church and her First Communion, St. Elizabeth Ann wrote in her journal: "At last GOD IS MINE and I AM HIS."[79] For the rest of her life, her deep faith and pioneering

79 Journal Entry of March 25, 1805, in *The Beauty of the Eucharist: Shaping and Sustaining Our Catholic Identity*, Eds. Rosemary Vaccari Mysel, Andrew J. Vaccari, Peter I. Vaccari. Boston: Pauline Books and Media (2005), p. 6.

service to the Church in our young nation was nourished by the Holy Eucharist.

55. In recent years, increasing numbers of Christians in our country have left their churches and become religiously unaffiliated. We invite Catholics who have left the Church or who no longer practice the faith to come home. We miss you and we love you. We pray that Jesus will draw you back to your Catholic family, his Mystical Body, through his Eucharistic Body. We repeat words attributed to St. Teresa of Calcutta: "Once you understand the Eucharist, you can never leave the Church. Not because the Church won't let you but because your heart won't let you."

SENT FORTH

56. Pope Benedict XVI reminded us that the "love that we celebrate in the sacrament is not something we can keep to ourselves. By its very nature it demands to be shared with all."[80] We are not the only ones in need of the love that Christ has shown us. We are called to help the rest of the world experience it. "What the world needs is God's love;

80 Pope Benedict XVI, *Sacramentum Caritatis*, no. 84.

it needs to encounter Christ and to believe in him. The Eucharist is thus the source and summit not only of the Church's life, but also of her mission."[81] Jesus is sent by the Father for the salvation of the world. At the very end of the celebration of the Eucharist, we who have received the Body and Blood of Christ and have been incorporated more profoundly into his Mystical Body are likewise sent out to proclaim the Good News for the salvation of the world: "Go in peace, glorifying the Lord by your life."

57. Pope Francis has insisted that evangelization—spreading the Good News of Jesus Christ—is a task that belongs to every member of the Church, not just a few specialists:

> All the baptized, whatever their position in the Church or their level of instruction in the faith, are agents of evangelization, and it would be insufficient to envisage a plan of evangelization to be carried out by professionals while the rest of the faithful would simply be passive recipients. The new evangelization calls for personal involvement on the part of each of the baptized.[82]

81 Pope Benedict XVI, *Sacramentum Caritatis*, no. 84.

82 Pope Francis, *Evangelii Gaudium*, no. 120.

He exhorts us all to become missionary disciples: "Every Christian is a missionary to the extent that he or she has encountered the love of God in Christ Jesus: we no longer say that we are 'disciples' and 'missionaries,' but rather that we are always 'missionary disciples.'"[83] What is essential is not that one have advanced training, but rather that one discover through Christ the love that God has for us and that one desire to lead others to that same joyful discovery: "[A]nyone who has truly experienced God's saving love does not need much time or lengthy training to go out and proclaim that love."[84] All that is needed is for one who has known that love—the love that is displayed most preeminently in the Eucharist—to tell other people about it.

> All of us are called to offer others an explicit witness to the saving love of the Lord, who despite our imperfections offers us his closeness, his word and his strength, and gives meaning to our lives. In your heart you know that it is not the same to live without him; what you have come to realize, what has helped you to live and given

83 Pope Francis, *Evangelii Gaudium*, no. 120.
84 Pope Francis, *Evangelii Gaudium*, no. 120.

you hope, is what you also need to communicate to others.[85]

58. We have offered these reflections on the Eucharistic faith and practice of the Church as a starting point. There is much more that could be said, but what is most important is that we enter more deeply by faith and love into this great Mystery of Mysteries. Let us all ask the Lord to call us into a time of Eucharistic renewal, a time of prayer and reflection, of acts of charity and sincere repentance. The Lord is with us in the Eucharistic Mystery celebrated in our parishes and missions, in our beautiful cathedrals and in our poorest chapels. He is present and he draws near to us, so that we can draw nearer to him. The Lord is generous to us with his grace; and so we, by his grace, should always humbly ask him to give us what we need.

59. *I am the Alpha and the Omega*, the Risen Christ says to us, *the beginning and the end. To the thirsty I will give a gift from the spring of life-giving water* (Rev

85 Pope Francis, *Evangelii Gaudium*, no. 121.

21:6). Brothers and sisters, let us thirst for the Lord who first suffered thirst for us (Jn 19:28). Let us adore Jesus who ever remains with us, on all the altars of the world, and lead others to share in our joy!